HOW THE WORLD MAKES MUSIC

BRASS INSTRUMENTS

by ANITA GANERI

A⁺

Smart Apple Media

Published by Smart Apple Media
P.O. Box 3263, Mankato, Minnesota 56002

Printed in the United States of America at Corporate Graphics, in North Mankato, Minnesota.

Library of Congress Cataloging-in-Publication Data
Ganeri, Anita, 1961-
Brass instruments / by Anita Ganeri.
    p. cm. — (How the world makes music)
Includes index.
Summary: "Describes various brass instruments from around the world, such as
the familiar trumpet and trombone, along with historical instruments such as
the Alphorn, serpent, and traditional instruments still played today, including the
didgeridoo and the dung-chen"—Provided by publisher.
ISBN 978-1-59920-477-2 (library binding)
1. Brass instruments—Juvenile literature. I. Title.
ML933.G36 2012
788.9'1922--dc22

                                                    2010053889

Created by Appleseed Editions, Ltd.
Designed by Guy Callaby
Illustrated by Graham Rosewarne
Edited by Jinny Johnson
Picture research by Su Alexander

DAD0047
3-2011

9 8 7 6 5 4 3 2 1

Contents

Brass Instruments

Modern brass instruments are played in bands, orchestras, and jazz bands. You will also hear them in movie scores. Brass instruments are played around the world and have been played for centuries.

This is the brass section of an orchestra, playing in a concert. The section includes trumpets, trombones, tubas, and horns.

Origins

Modern brass instruments are made from metal. This is how they get their name. But they have their origins in many instruments made from lots of different materials, including shell, horn, and hollow branches. What all these instruments have in common is that the player uses his or her lips to produce the sound.

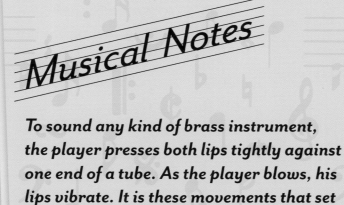

Musical Notes

To sound any kind of brass instrument, the player presses both lips tightly against one end of a tube. As the player blows, his lips vibrate. It is these movements that set the air inside the instrument vibrating to produce sounds.

Ancient Trumpets

People were playing simple trumpets as long as 3,500 years ago. Many ancient Egyptian pictures show people playing trumpets while leading armies of marching soldiers. Two ancient trumpets were found in King Tutankhamun's tomb when it was discovered in 1922. (Tutankhamun had died around 1323 BC.) One trumpet was made from silver, the other from bronze.

Musical Notes

In 1939, a trumpeter was allowed to play Tutankhamun's silver trumpet. A recording was made of the sound. Sadly, the force of the trumpeter's breath shattered the ancient instrument! (It has since been put back together again.)

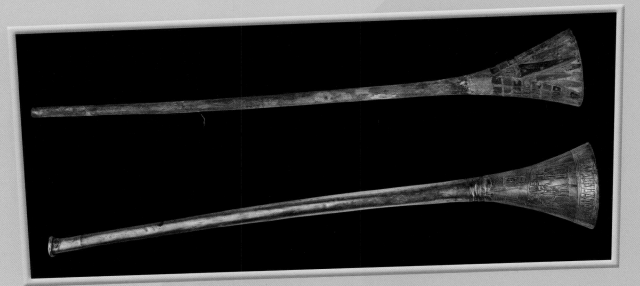

These are two ancient trumpets found in Tutankhamun's tomb. They may have been used to send signals during battles.

War Trumpets

The noise of trumpets was used in ancient times by armies to frighten their enemies. One of these war trumpets was the carynx, played by the Celts. This metal instrument was topped with an open-mouthed animal head to make it even more alarming.

This is a modern version of a carynx.

Large Trumpets

The didgeridoo is a type of large trumpet that is played by the Aboriginal people of Australia. It is made from the hollowed-out branch of a eucalyptus tree. Traditionally, the branches were buried in the ground and left to be hollowed out by termites.

Musical Notes

The didgeridoo is played by blowing hard through vibrating lips. As the player squeezes air from his mouth down the tube, he also breathes in through his nose. This is called circular breathing. It allows the player to keep the sound going continuously.

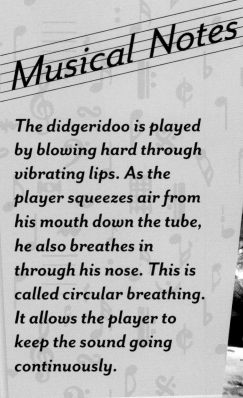

Alphorns were originally used to send messages across long distances in the mountains.

Alphorn

The alphorn is a gigantic instrument that is traditionally played in the mountains of Switzerland. It is carved out of wood and can be up to 16 feet (5 m) long.

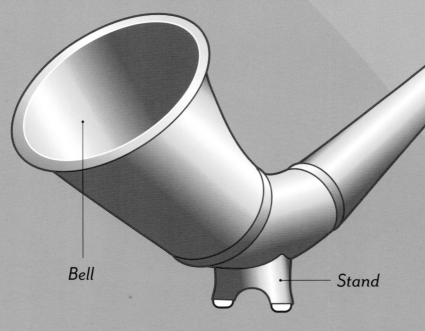

Bell

Stand

Sounding Signals

Trumpets have been used throughout history to send signals. Players could only produce a few notes on simple trumpets, but the sound was loud and clear. In ancient Peru, the Moche people made trumpets out of clay. Other trumpets were made from bone, bark, and wood.

A young boy plays a trumpet made from animal horn in Ethiopia, Africa. The sound of this trumpet can carry over a long distance.

Dung-Chen

The dung-chen is a Tibetan trumpet. It is made out of brass or copper. It can be up to 10 feet (3 m) long, but it is built in sections that collapse to make it shorter for storage.

Bell

Mouthpiece

Dung-chen are usually played in pairs. They are linked with the Buddhist religion. Their sound signals the start of important rituals, as well as dawn and sunset.

Musical Notes

The dung-chen produces a very, very low sound. When two of these instruments are played together in the high mountain valleys of Tibet, the echoing noise can be quite eerie.

Trumpet

The trumpet has a bright and brilliant sound. It can be clearly heard even when the whole band is playing. Trumpets are also played in jazz bands, military bands, and orchestras.

The members of a military band have to learn to play their instruments while they are marching. Military bands also include some wind and percussion instruments.

Changing Notes

Trumpet players make some notes by changing the shape made by their lips. The trumpet also has three valves. These allow the player to make other notes. When the player presses down one of the valves, it connects to an extra set of tubing. This means the vibrating air has farther to travel, and the note sounded is lower.

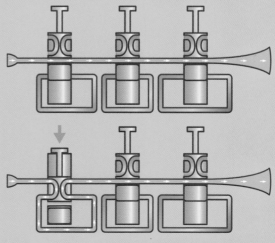

Musical Notes

The trumpet is often played in jazz music. Louis Armstrong was one of the most famous jazz trumpeters. He came from New Orleans, Louisiana. His nickname was Satchmo (short for Satchelmouth), because of his wide mouth and big grin.

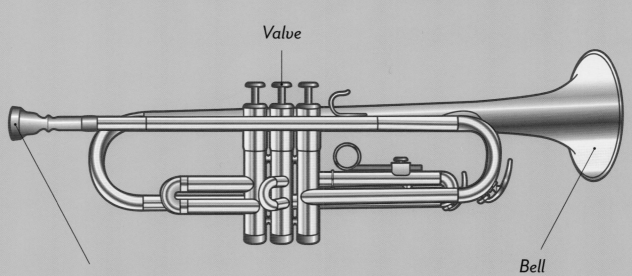

Valve

Mouthpiece

Bell

Trombone

The trombone has a deeper and richer sound than the trumpet. It also has an unusual way of producing different notes. The trombone player makes some notes by changing the shape of his lips. But other notes are made by moving a piece of tubing in and out of the instrument. This tubing is called a slide.

A person who plays a trombone is called a trombonist or trombone player. Trombones are played in many different kinds of music, from classical to folk and pop.

The Slide

The trombone slide is a U-shaped tube with a crossbar. The player holds the crossbar with his right hand to move the slide in and out. With the slide pushed out, the tubing is much longer than with the slide pulled back in. The farther the vibrating air has to travel through the tube, the deeper the note.

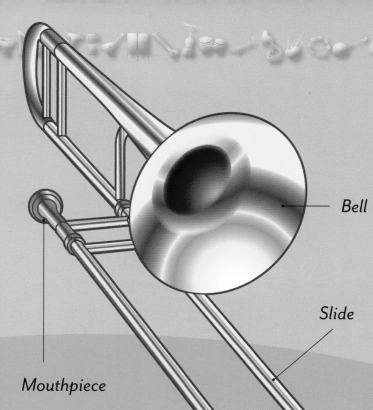

Bell

Slide

Mouthpiece

Musical Notes

Brass players can use devices called mutes to alter the sound of their instruments.

A mute fits snugly into the end of the instrument and makes the sound quieter. Different mutes also have different effects on the sound. Some mutes give a more piercing noise; others make a buzzing sound.

Mute

Ancient Horns

In ancient times, people made musical instruments from the horns of animals, such as cows and sheep. They simply cut a small hole in the end of the horn, then blew through the horn to produce a sound. In Africa, people often cut a hole into the side of the horn. They blew across this hole to produce a sound.

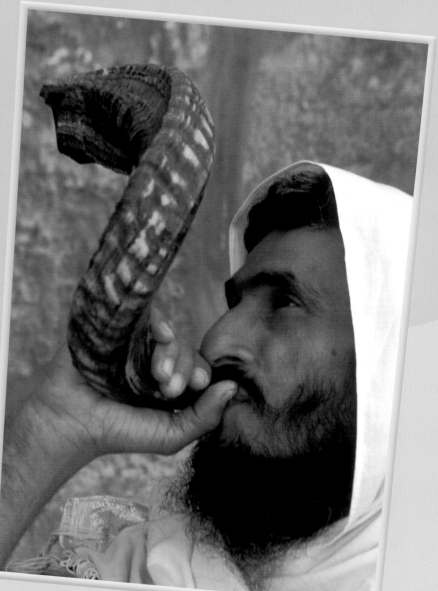

This Jewish man is blowing a shofar. In ancient times, it announced important events, such as the arrival of the king.

Shofar

The shofar is a special horn used in the Jewish religion. It is usually made from the horn of a ram. It is still played on important days in the Jewish religious calendar, such as Rosh Hashanah (the Jewish New Year) and Yom Kippur (the Day of Atonement).

Some ancient horns were not made from horns at all. Simple horns were made from clay and wood, large shells, and even out of armadillo tails! This boy is blowing a large shell of a conch, a kind of sea creature, which gives a low, deep sound.

Ivory Horns

In medieval times, some horns were carved out of elephant ivory. Only very wealthy people could afford such luxurious horns. These ivory horns were called oliphants.

The Savernake Horn is made from ivory and decorated with silver. It is engraved with animals, including a lion and a unicorn. The horn was last blown in 1940.

The Savernake Horn

Ivory horns were carried by nobles to sound signals when they were out hunting. This hunting horn gets its name from the Savernake Forest in Wiltshire, England. It was made in the 1300s, and it is decorated with silver bands.

Musical Notes

The name "oliphant" comes from an ancient word for elephant. The ivory used to make oliphants usually came from elephants.

Musical Notes

Some ancient musical instruments can still be played today. The sounds of the lur are heard on several CDs that have been made by Scandinavian brass players.

A lur is an ancient Scandinavian horn made from bronze. It has a long curved tube topped by a flat disc. Many of these instruments have been dug out of boggy ground in Denmark and other parts of southern Scandinavia. Lurs were usually played in pairs.

This statue shows a pair of lur blowers. A lur is around 7 feet (2 m) long and has a curved handle to make it easier to carry. The lur was probably sounded in battles to frighten the enemy and send signals to troops.

19

Bugle

The bugle is a simple metal horn that has no valves. Bugle players sound different notes by changing the shape of their lips. This means that bugles can play only a few notes.

Since the eighteenth century, armies have used bugles to send signals. Different patterns of notes, or "calls," sent messages to soldiers on the battlefield.

Mouthpiece

Bell

Bugle Calls

There were many different bugle calls and each had its own meaning. For example, one call was sounded to tell the soldiers to "go forward." Another meant "cease fire." Bugle calls were also used in camp to tell soldiers when to wake up, or to signal meal times.

Musical Notes

At military funerals and at ceremonies to remember those who have died in battle, a bugler plays a famous call, known as Taps. This call was originally used to signal the end of the day to soldiers in camp.

French Horn

French horns add a beautiful mellow tone to orchestras, concert bands, and brass bands. The French horn has lots of loops and coils of tubing that end in a wide opening, called the bell. The player holds the horn by placing the right hand inside the bell.

Mouthpiece

Tubes

Bell

Valves

Two in One

This is a single French horn. There are also double horns, where one set of tubes plays lower notes, and another set plays higher, brighter notes. The player uses an extra valve to switch between the two.

Learning to play the French horn takes lots of practice! Players need to get their fingering, blowing, and breathing techniques right so that they can make a smooth sound.

Musical Notes

There are usually four horns in an orchestra. But when German composer Richard Strauss wrote his Alpine Symphony, he included parts for 20 horns! (His father was a horn player.)

Tuba

The brass section of a band or orchestra is made up of trumpets, trombones, French horns, and tubas. The tuba is the biggest instrument, and it makes the deepest sounds. Tubas are also played in military bands.

These are tuba players in a military band. Tubas are also played in jazz, classical, and big band music.

Sitting and Marching

In an orchestra, tuba players sit on chairs and rest the instruments on their laps. Some tubas for marching are designed to rest on the player's shoulder. The bell points forward instead of upward.

Mouthpipe

Bell

Valve tube

Valves

Musical Notes

The Sousaphone is named after bandmaster John Philip Sousa. It is a kind of tuba that fits around the body of the player, with the bell pointing forward above the player's head. It is very popular in marching bands.

Brass Bands

Marching bands and brass bands have many different types of brass instruments. In British brass bands, the instrument that plays the melody is the cornet. The cornet is like a trumpet, but it is shorter and has a softer sound. Cornets are also played in marching bands.

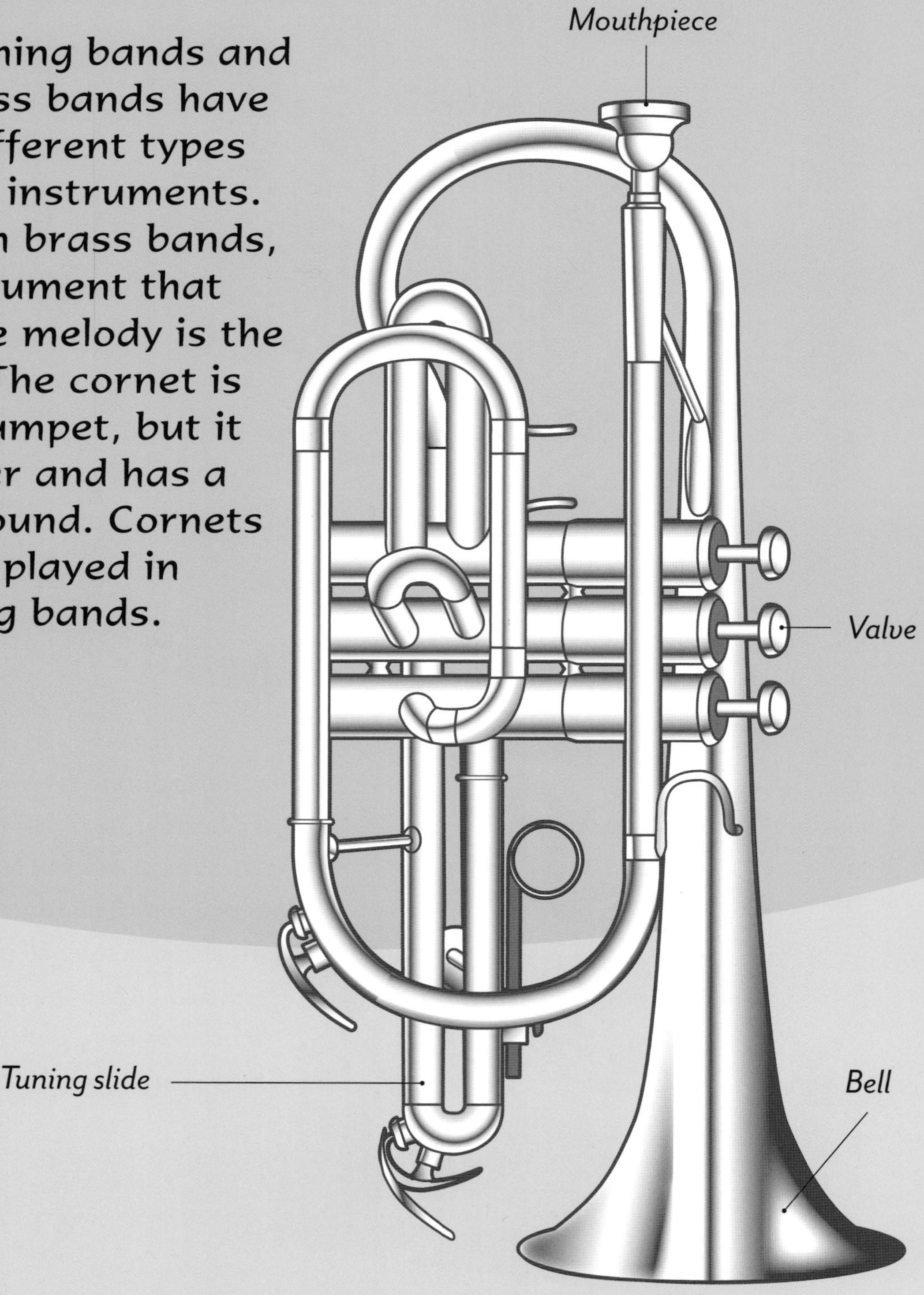

Mouthpiece

Valve

Tuning slide

Bell

Flügelhorn and Euphonium

The flügelhorn is like a cornet, but it has a wider tube and bigger bell. This means that it makes a darker sound than the cornet. The euphonium is popular in brass bands and marching bands. It is like a small tuba, and it has a rich, velvety sound.

The euphonium can be played as part of a band, orchestra, or as a solo instrument. Many euphonium players play other brass instruments too, such as trumpets.

Musical Notes

Other brass instruments played in bands include alto horns, mellophones, bass trombones, and baritones. Concert bands also feature a percussion section and wind instruments.

Serpent

The serpent is a strange instrument that is a cross between a brass and a wind instrument. With its winding shape, it certainly lives up to its name. It was invented in France in the 1590s.

This serpent was made in about 1820 from pearwood, leather, brass, and ivory.

Wooden Snake

The serpent's curved body is made from wood, with six finger holes in two groups of three. It has a metal mouthpiece, similar to that of a trombone. In the 1600s and 1700s, the serpent was played in churches and then it became popular in military bands. It was eventually replaced by instruments such as the tuba and the euphonium.

Musical Notes

The serpent had a cousin called the ophicleide. This instrument was developed in the 1800s. Unlike the serpent, it was made from metal and it had keys instead of finger holes. Its name combines the Greek words for "serpent" and "key."

Words to Remember

Aboriginal
The Aboriginals were the first people to live in Australia, many thousands of years ago.

bell
In a brass instrument, the bell is the bell-shaped end of the tube.

brass
a metal that is a mixture of two other metals—copper and zinc

Buddhist
a person who follows the teaching of the Buddha, a holy man who lived in India thousands of years ago

Celts
people who lived in Britain, France, and Spain before the Romans

clay
soft earth or mud that is molded into shape, then baked hard

copper
a reddish-brown metal

horn
Animal horn was once used to make many objects, including musical instruments.

ivory
the material that an elephant's tusks are made from

marching band
a band that marches as it plays, in time to the music

mouthpiece
In a brass instrument, the mouthpiece is the end of the tube that a player blows down.

mute
a device placed in the bell of a brass instrument to make the sound quieter

percussion instruments
musical instruments that are played by striking, such as drums, cymbals, and tambourines

score
the music played to accompany a film or stage play

slide
a piece of tubing on a trombone

termites
tiny, ant-like creatures known for chewing wood

valve
in a brass instrument, a device that a player presses to alter the length of the tube and the sound of the note

vibrations
when something, such as air, moves back and forth very quickly

wind instruments
musical instruments played by blowing across a reed or hole, such as flutes, clarinets, and oboes

Web Sites

Horn History from Horn Central
http://www.horncentral.com/Ancient_Brass_History.html

How Brass Instruments Work
http://www.method-behind-the-music.com/mechanics/brass

San Francisco Symphony Kids: Instruments of the Orchestra
http://www.sfskids.org/templates/instorchframe.asp?pageid=3

Sphinx Kids! Instrument Storage Room
http://www.sphinxkids.org/Instrument_Storage.html

Index

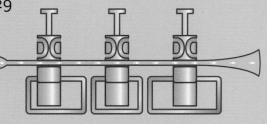